YOUR KNOWLEDGE HAS VALUE

Boğaç Aybey

German war literature. How effective did anti-war and anti-Nazism writers articulate themselves?

GRIN Publishing

Bibliographic information published by the German National Library:

The German National Library lists this publication in the National Bibliography; detailed bibliographic data are available on the Internet at http://dnb.dnb.de .

Imprint:

Copyright © 2013 GRIN Verlag GmbH
Print and binding: Books on Demand GmbH, Norderstedt Germany
ISBN: 978-3-656-90832-6

This book at GRIN:

http://www.grin.com/en/e-book/293379/german-war-literature-how-effective-did-anti-war-and-anti-nazism-writers

GRIN - Your knowledge has value

Since its foundation in 1998, GRIN has specialized in publishing academic texts by students, college teachers and other academics as e-book and printed book. The website www.grin.com is an ideal platform for presenting term papers, final papers, scientific essays, dissertations and specialist books.

Visit us on the internet:

http://www.grin.com/

http://www.facebook.com/grincom

http://www.twitter.com/grin_com

German War Literature:

How effective did anti-war and-Nazism writers articulate themselves?

Boğaç Aybey

English Department

Research Rough Draft

07 January 2013

Boğaç Aybey

English Department

Research Rough Draft

07 January 2013

German War Literature:

How effective did anti-war and-Nazism writers articulate themselves?

Historical time periods are in most cases themes of literature and inspire writers; to express their opinions; to reflect these periods ; and to enlighten people. So literature and history have been always grown together interdependently. Similarly, one of the most inspireful era is time interval between World War I and II. As the narrator of Böll's satire, *Christmas Not Just Once a Year* writes, war had enormous effect on the writers of wartime:

> During the years 1939 to 1945 there was a war on. In wartime there is a lot of
>
> singing, shooting, talking, fighting, starving and dying -- and bombs are
>
> dropped, all disagreeable things with which I have no intention of boring my
>
> contemporaries. I must merely mention them because the war had a bearing
>
> on the story I wish to tell (qtd. in Reid 2).

Almost every German artist wanted to articulate his/her view on war in different ways, but how exactly did they raise their voices? Nevertheless, their views of wartime differ. On the one hand, some authors wrote against either Nazi ideology or war; while on the other hand some writers wrote in favor of either Nazi regime or war. However, German writers against Hitler or war articulated themselves better, because even though it is prohibited to write against the government, they were courageous enough to criticize leaders and to discuss people's attitudes and point of views towards war, and the conditions of wartime.

Most important act of these writers was satirically criticizing on how the leaders

1

faltered their lands. In such restricted environment, they did not want to explicitly comment on why the leaders failed and which features of leaders deceived people, yet they achieved to convey their opinions effectively. Exemplarily, Bertolt Brecht writes in his poem "Hitler-Chorale" "Now thank we all the Lord/Who sent us Adolf Hitler" (qtd. in Ewen 286). It seems that Brecht actually praises Hitler "who'll clear away the dirt" as the poem continues, but why would he want to do that even though he compares Hitler's helpful big mouth with a weapon and a shield as the poem continues with "So great a help was his big mouth, /A weapon and a shield …" (286)? Mostly he wanted to conceal his satire and to be seen as if he praises Hitler, yet he wants to mean the other way. Probably, under the oppression of Nazi government, the best and most effective way was to inexplicably express one's ideas. So he did not want to directly give his message to the reader, and thus chose a satirical way to write his poems under the control of Nazis. In this sense, one cannot deny the reality that Hitler's big mouth manipulated big audiences in order them to participate in war. Probably his mouth was more useful than a weapon, because it did not only lead death of people, but it brought dirt to the Germany and German reputation. What Brecht asserts is the opposite of what Gerard Shuhmann argues in "Lied der Kämpfer"'s last strophe "Those of us now marching in the iron columns do so without questioning. /We are the fist of the Führer" (qtd. in Murdoch 107). However, in Shuhmann's view, people must accept what Hitler's big mouth was saying without hesitation, whereas Brecht warns the reader that Hitler gets what he wants by talking nonsense and will corrupt the nation. Also what Shuhmann suggests should not be the way an educated person, especially a poet, should think. Since an educated person should question and should not believe in everything especially the leaders say, one should acknowledge Brecht's satire against both how easily people believed in Hitler and how Hitler's big mouth affected crowds of people.

Similar to Brecht, Thomas Mann also discusses the hypnotizing effect of leaders and the eventual reaction against this by the citizens. In *Mario and the Magician*, Mann wants to convey how leaders in general entailed to fail, by showing that after charlatan, Cipolla, hypnotizes Mario in order to kiss him, Mario becomes conscious again and kills Cipolla with a piston (qtd. in Robertson 111). Mann wants to show that no matter how these leaders or charlatans manipulate people, people will be soon conscious again. What Mario does is a rebellious act, which many German writers one way or another achieved too, because by continuing to write no matter what the leaders made it impossible to do, they wanted to abolish the effect of the leaders which prevented the people to become conscious. Also by doing this, they called every German intellectual to spread the truth.

Another important act against war was to criticize people's changing attitudes during wartime. To do so, German writer's reflected people's thoughts and how people perceived everything that belongs to wartime. Hence Brecht's protagonist soldier of Drums in the Night ,Andreas Kragler, faces with animosity from his people. His fiancé's father, Balicke, refers Andreas "Beasts. Beasts. If anyone asks, Why beasts? You eat human flesh, and you must be crushed." (qtd. in Ewen 106). By discussing the meaning of soldiers, Brecht wanted to criticize people's changing attitudes towards soldiers. In making this criticism, Brecht basically warned his readers that even Nazi poets called young men to war fields, one cannot deny the effects of war on these men. When soldiers come to their hometowns, they feel alienated from their people. This is not the only effect, but even they must be the ones that should be extolled, soldiers are abased as if they haven't done anything for their country. Additionally, by showing how others react to Andreas differently than most readers would have predicted, Brecht claims that people who are not courageous enough to fight denounce soldiers. On the other hand, in Nazi poets' view, going to war was something holy and these young men became heroes during war fields as favorite writer of the Nazis, Stefan George,

3

argues "the new Germany was a place for heroes and force" (Waller 224). Heroes he means only consisted of "man he exalted" not the "woman he degraded" (224). Heroic act is therefore, something they encourage people to commit. Brecht actually took his side against Nazi poets and as a reaction, Brecht refutes George's attitude towards heroism in the war fields, by showing the unwelcoming, degrading attitude of Andreas' people.

Other different aspect of change in people's attitudes is the effect of corruption on the personal relationships. In *The Excursion of the Dead Girl*, Anna Seghers creates every character for different solid purposes. Every character has pieces of war in them and is affected by Hitler's regime, relinquishes old friendships and starts to judge others. As Seghers writes, by willingly abiding by the laws Marianne puts her effort so that Hitler and the new movement succeed. Marianne's husband Gustav Liebig, who has a leadership position as an "SS-man", encourages other people to believe in "Hitler's one Volk". Marianne provokes Gustav, when he reports Leni's husband Fritz, who defies joining SS and participates in illegal printing (Maier-Katkin). People like Marianne and Gustav, prioritize state and for them friendship and empathy have less value. Once-close friends, Leni and Marianne, as a result of war, become separated and their relationships cannot be the same as before the war. People like Marianne who support Hitler sells their friends in order to be seen law-abiding and orthodox to Nazi ideology. However, Seghers maintains that even though Marianne and Gustav steadfastly believe in everything Hitler says and approves, at the end, they are killed like every other supporters of Hitler.

Other point Seghers tries to impose is the Aryan race against Jewish conflict that led the relationships between different races to deteriorate. German people segregated Jewish people and whenever they saw Jews, they insulted them. In Seghers' view, this conflict is way too pointless, because it deteriorated relationships between close friends. This change in relationships can be observed in *The Excursion of the Dead Girl*, when Nora supports new

4

racial laws that designate to differentiate the Aryan Germans from Jews. Even though she used to adore Jewish teacher Miss Sichel, she and her classmates immediately start calling her belittling names like "Jewish Pig" (qtd in Maier-Katkin). Seghers' characters thus are victims of race difference and hypnotizing effect of Hitler and Nazi socialism. Characters affected by Hitler see the world as black and white because they are under the influence of Hitler. As a result, even though the characters are in favor of Hitler, they are obliged to death too. This way, Seghers emphasizes that such a mentality that Hitler imposes on the citizens is mal-functioning. However, according to Gottfried Benn, a nationalist poet, in order to maintain "The Order", one must follow the "principle of Race" and he asserts that German Youth scarified himself for this purpose (Frank 117). Benn is mistaken in his view that only one race-Aryan Race-, pure German blood, must prevail in one country especially in Germany, because he overlooks the fact that it would only lead to a society that lacks humanity, close feelings and generous attitude towards other races. As Benn would not agree upon, Seghers insists upon that cold bloodily betraying close friends and bias against Jews will bring German nation nowhere.

Addition to people's alternating manners, Anti-Nazi artists also warned people that nationalist attitude of countries could not lead the nations to a better place. To show his irritation, in *Mario and the Magician* by Thomas Mann, a family becomes irritated by "xenophobic and nationalist attitudes of Italians" and wants to end their holiday in Mussolini's Italy (Robertson 111). Mussolini's Italy's attitude is an inexplicable reference to other nationalist countries -especially to Germany. Not being able to directly criticize Germany, Mann chooses to comment on Italy meaning actually Germany. Contrary, Nazi poets like Heinrich Anacker, calls people "to arms rather than a call to political unity" (Murdoch 106-7). "When we are marching and singing, with firm step and tread /what, are you not with us, brother? /The cry is urgent in your ear, too: 'You must join, too!'" (qtd. in

Murdoch 106-7). They wanted the German nation to unite and become as one. This nationalist attitude was also same in Italy and other countries. Mann clearly shows how he repudiated this attitude in any sense, because according to him, this urgent cry was irritating and unwelcoming and people had to welcome each other no matter from which country they come. Nazi poets' claim to form a nationalist and united Germany is therefore questionable. In his view, Murdoch's attitude is to fail and people would soon become annoyed by this ethos.

Another damage Hitler left behind in people's attitude was propaganda for children. Literary material and posters had major effects on both children's minds and attitudes. Children exposed this propaganda even in books. In 1940 in Germany, child's first reading book has been officially published and contained one passage targets to "Jungvolk— the most junior branch of the Nazi youth movement, for ten- to fourteen-year-olds": "Here they come with their brown shirts... We salute the flag and shout: Heil Hitler! How well they march! How loudly and clearly they sing 'Our Banner Waves Before Us!' " (qtd. in Murdoch 101-2). Nationalism and sense of war wanted to be imposed on children's minds. In other words, they believed that children from early stage of their lives must be manipulated by using literature. By describing how merrily Nazi youth celebrate Hitler and his soldiers, Nazi writers explicitly wanted to divert the children' energy and focus to the war and Nazi ideology. Nazi writers were in some points right when they wanted their youth to become aware of the war. However they were not fully aware how they transformed the youth into an emotionless, cold-blooded and savage crowd.

As a reaction to Nazi propagandists, Anna Seghers questions children's eagerness to participate in war. School children in *The Excursion of the Dead Girls* are excited to participate in war and adventures, because they get bored of their serene life where nothing happens. Their main inspiration is the war stories that they heart from the previous generation:

"... the modest comfort of every work day seemed to repulse the children, so that they soon took in eagerly their fathers' war reports and longed ... for uniforms" (qtd in Maier-Katkin). Children are exposed to war stories, propaganda and etc. and become more evil during the book. Parents in this book are ineffective in terms of teaching "certain moral values regarding community life" (Maier-Katkin). "Instead of reminding the children that communities can be based on tolerance, respect, and the right of every human being to dignity", they do not take notice of their tendency towards war, adventure and nationalism (Maier-Katkin). Basically Seghers warns that one has to be aware of where youth is going. Even though Nazi writers wanted to inform youth about war, one cannot deny that they overused propaganda. Parent's oblivion is thus a reference to the awareness of the society how much this propaganda affected their youth. Thus one has to concur with Seghers that over-exposure of nationalist propaganda combining oblivion of the society to the savagery of the youth caused what Nazi writers would have not predicted.

Last significant act of most German writers was to express war memories, conditions during wartime and damage of war in his/her own unique way. The melancholic atmosphere of this era was usually criticized by showing different aspects of wartime. Some writers are in the opinion that war is faulty and empty, and bring the nations nowhere. Theodor Plievier's novel about the German naval riot in 1917, *Des Kaiser's Kulis* states :"We are not fighting for the Fatherland, nor for German honour. We are dying for ignorance and for the millionaires" (qtd. in Murdoch 6). In Plievier's view, Germany was in war not because Hitler cared much about either prosperity or honor of Germany. However, according to him, ignorant Germany took place in war, because of greed and ambitions of politicians especially Hitler. Thus Plievier wants the reader to realize how severe the conditions of war were, and one had to be unbounded from the ignorance that was imposed on the citizens as a result of Hitler's manipulative attitude. On the other hand, Stefan George wrote in his poem:

Too late for patience and the cure.

Ten thousand must the holy madness seize;

Ten thousand must the holy pestilence slay,

Ten thousand the holy war. (qtd. in Waller 224)

For him, war can cure the land slowly. According to his view, "The new Germany was a place for heroes and force. Too late for peace; too late for liberalism." (Waller 224). George predominantly is on the opinion that war is actually meaningful and as a result, he perceived the war as a spiritual salvation for the land. Writers in favor of war and Nazi Germany wanted to make war seem affirmative. Thus they basically promoted war and wanted to show that Hitler's ideology was something everyone should follow. By focusing only on the advantages of war on the country, George overlooks the tremendous effect of war on citizens and soldiers. He only focuses on the new Germany and how soldiers and war will shape Germany's future. As he insists, war and rival countries have damage on the honor of Germany, and he takes defeat in this war as a matter of honor. He insists that victory is essential for the land and thus he gives meaning to war. On the other hand, one has to concur with Plievier that war did not bring Germany neither honor nor prosperity, because a lot of soldiers and citizens died without knowing why they fought and died.

Similar to the discussion of meaning of war, Brecht in "To Posterity" questions reliability of war: "For we went changing countries more often/ than our shoes, / In the class war, despairing/ When there was only injustice and no indignation." (qtd. in Ewen 330). He concludes that everything changes at wartime and nothing is granted. Also Brecht wittily depicts the atmosphere and situation of wartime. In wartime, borders of countries can be changeable and one cannot talk about justice. Basically Brecht raises the question that if in wartime there is such alternation and lack of human dignity, does war bring anything not despairing for humankind? Additionally, in Mann's *Doktor Faustus*, while Leverkühn studies theology, he has an attempt to study the "atmosphere of the Faust legend", but then he decides to learn music. Mainly, "Dr. Faustus is Germany, the collapse of which is symbolized in the last musical works of Leverkühn, Apocalipsis cumfiguris and Wehklag Dr. Fausti."(Bithell 341). Mann uses Faust, Goethe's play in which an evil wants to deceive a wise person to provide him longer life, as his background for Doktor Faustus. Germany was swept into war with expectations of prosperity and honor, but instead only damage and empty promises, similar to evil's empty promises in Faust. Since all of the promises war leave on people is nothing but collapse that tragically can be expressed with music in the background. Contrary, writers, who encourage people to fight for their countries' honor, misses the point that at wartime nothing is crystal clear and   there is no point in fighting when one knows that fighting will only bring the evil spirit of humankind. Contrary, Mann and Brecht deplore the idea of the opponent side by showing them that countries entail to collapse and uncertainty as a result of war.

Addition to the emptiness and unreliability of war, German writers perceive war something they suffered and cannot get rid of those memories. They depict war as an illness and effects of war is so malicious and disease-like, that one cannot get through it quickly. Brecht writes in *Drums in the Night*: "Can you get rid of the army or of the good Lord? Can you get rid of all the pain and suffering man has taught the Devil? No, you can't get rid of it, but you can drink whiskey." (qtd. in Ewen 99). According to Brecht, if Devil had learnt lesson from mankind, then war and concepts related to war are actually only deceptive and corruptive. It basically means that humans are more dangerous and devious than devil. Yet Brecht's claim is exaggerating though one has to admit that bombs, execution of Jews, death of soldiers and citizens are things that even devil cannot manipulate people to do. So killing his own kind and sad war memories hit the people at first and realizing that they could not change the fact that what happened could not be recovered led them to desolation and seeking

9

for salvation. Ironically, Brecht suggests to drink whiskey ,because the damage has been already done and nothing can make the pain go away from the memories of the people. Similarly, Brecht writes in "Puntila and His Servant Matti":

> This is the year they will speak of.
>
> This is the year they will not speak of.
>
> The old see the young one dying.
>
> The foolish see the wise dying.
>
> Earth no longer bears; she swallows.
>
> Heaven no longer sends down rain but steel. (qtd. in Ewen 329)

By using contradictions in his poem, Brecht points out that due to war, that of nobody want to speak and to remember, nations lost educated young soldiers. In other words, he believes that nations could not bear the burden of the cruelty of war, the steel, and because they could not stop or did not intend to stop, war has been a part of the routine and nations became accustomed to the state of wartime and suffer.

Besides of the consequences of war on people's memories and conditions of countries, during wartime freedom of thought and expression of individuals were limited by Nazi government. Brecht criticizes effect of Hitler's regime on poets in "In finstern Zeiten": "In days to come they will not say:/ The times were dark./ But: Why were the poets silent?"(qtd. in Ewen 291). Brecht urges poets and writers to express themselves and to raise their voices against the injustice of war even though Hitler government oppressed writers not to write opinions against Nazis. In these dark times, which mean both the war and limitation of individuals, his poem can be considered as an act of defiance. Additionally, Brecht in "To Posterity" expresses his thoughts on restrictions of writers:

> A guileless word is folly. A smooth forehead
>
> Betokens insensitiveness. He who laughs

Has not yet heard.

The terrible news.

What an age is this,

When to speak of trees is almost a crime,

For it is silence about innumerable outrages (qtd. in Ewen 330)

According to Nazis, one must avoid expressing one's opinion and not feeling the same way as Nazis. Freedom of expression was limited and being sensitive, guileless contradicts with Nazis' cold-blooded and deceitful manners. In his another poem "General, That Tank" Bertolt Brecht writes :

General, a man is a useful creature.

He can fly, and he can kill.

But he has one failing:

He can think. (qtd. in Hamburger, Middleton 117)

Brecht actually criticizes Nazis' view of human, because Nazis perceived human as a cold-blooded war machine that kills his own kind and neither thinks nor questions. These features that fit with Nazi ideology made human a functional machine only for use in war. Thus in Brecht's view Nazis overlooked the fact that by thinking about what is going on in their land, people can become conscious again. One can support his view that human's thinking ability cannot be taken away from them.

All in all, in a time period where it was easier for Nazi writers to promote their opinions, anti-Nazi writers did not stop holding onto their believes and expressing themselves by pushing the limits. Thus anti-Nazi and–war writers are products of their era as a result of both Hitler and war. These writers have grown with the history and became more mature in their art as defiance to the history they could not bare. If they have not seen that much of desolation and cruelty, could they be able to express themselves so creatively? Could writers like Brecht, Mann and others be able to raise their voices in their authentic ways? Probably, there would be writers like them but could they be courageous to try to enlighten the citizens and to criticize the points they did not agree? What these writers achieved can be considered as inspiration for the modern writers and the prose of these writers can be a unique way for modern writers to emulate.

Works Cited

Bithell, Jethro, ed. Germany, a Companion to German Studies. 5th ed. London: Methuen, 1955.

    Questia School. Print.

Ewen, Frederic. Bertolt Brecht: His Life, His Art, and His times. New York: Carol Pub. Group, 1992.

    Print.

Frank, Joseph. Responses to Modernity: Essays in the Politics of Culture. New York: Fordham UP,

    2012. Questia School. Print.

Hamburger, Michael, and Christopher Middleton, eds. Modern German Poetry, 1910-1960. New

    York: Grove, 1962. Questia School. 16 Dec. 2012. Print.

Maier-Katkin, Birgit. "Writing for Memory: Anna Seghers, History, Literature, and Complicity in the

    Third Reich." CLIO 31.4 (2002): 367+. Questia School. Print.

Murdoch, Brian. Fighting Songs and Warring Words : Popular Lyrics of Two WorldWars. London, GBR:

    Routledge, 1990. Ebrary.Print.

Reid, J.H. "Private and Public Filters: Memories of War in Heinrich Böll's Fiction and Nonfiction". In

    European Memories of the Second World War (pp. 2-10). Burdett, Charles, Claire Gorrara,

    and Helmut Peitsch, eds. New York: Berghahn, 1999. Questia School. Print.

Robertson, Ritchie, ed. The Cambridge Companion to Thomas Mann. Cambridge, England: Cambridge

    UP, 2001. Questia School. Print.

Waller, Willard, ed. War in the Twentieth Century. New York: Dryden, 1940. Questia School. Print.